W9-AKV-437

Put Beginning Readers on the Right Track with
ALL ABOARD READING™

The All Aboard Reading series is especially designed for beginning readers. Written by noted authors and illustrated in full color, these are books that children really want to read—books to excite their imagination, expand their interests, make them laugh, and support their feelings. With fiction and nonfiction stories that are high interest and curriculum-related, All Aboard Reading books offer something for every young reader. And with four different reading levels, the All Aboard Reading series lets you choose which books are most appropriate for your children and their growing abilities.

Picture Readers
Picture Readers have super-simple texts, with many nouns appearing as rebus pictures. At the end of each book are 24 flash cards—on one side is a rebus picture; on the other side is the written-out word.

Station Stop 1
Station Stop 1 books are best for children who have just begun to read. Simple words and big type make these early reading experiences more comfortable. Picture clues help children to figure out the words on the page. Lots of repetition throughout the text helps children to predict the next word or phrase—an essential step in developing word recognition.

Station Stop 2
Station Stop 2 books are written specifically for children who are reading with help. Short sentences make it easier for early readers to understand what they are reading. Simple plots and simple dialogue help children with reading comprehension.

Station Stop 3
Station Stop 3 books are perfect for children who are reading alone. With longer text and harder words, these books appeal to children who have mastered basic reading skills. More complex stories captivate children who are ready for more challenging books.

In addition to All Aboard Reading books, look for All Aboard Math Readers™ (fiction stories that teach math concepts children are learning in school) and All Aboard Science Readers™ (nonfiction books that explore the most fascinating science topics in age-appropriate language).

All Aboard for happy reading!

AN ALL ABOARD READING™

COLLECTION

Simply Science

Grosset & Dunlap

The All Aboard Station Stop 1 Collection:
SIMPLY SCIENCE published in 2003.

WATER. Text copyright © 2002 by Emily Neye. Illustrations copyright © 2002 by Cindy Revell.
TURTLES. Text copyright © 2003 by Jodi Huelin. Illustrations copyright © 2003 by
Pedro Julio Gonzalez. STARS. Text copyright © 1996 by Jennifer Dussling. Illustrations copyright
© 1996 by Mavis Smith. SPIDER'S LUNCH. Text copyright © 1995 by Joanna Cole.
Illustrations copyright © 1995 by Ron Broda. FROGS. Text copyright © 1998 by Laura Driscoll.
Illustrations copyright © 1998 by Judith Moffatt. BUTTERFLIES. Text copyright © 2000 by
Emily Neye. Illustrations © 2000 by Ron Broda. SHARKS. Text copyright © 2001 by Ginjer Clarke.
Illustrations © 2001 by Steven James Petruccio. All rights reserved.

Published by Grosset & Dunlap, a division of Penguin Young Readers Group,
345 Hudson Street, New York, NY, 10014.
ALL ABOARD and GROSSET & DUNLAP are trademarks of Penguin Group (USA) Inc.
Published simultaneously in Canada. Printed in the U.S.A.

ISBN 0-448-43336-2   A B C D E F G H I J

An All Aboard Reading™ Collection

Station Stop 1

Collection

Simply Science

By Ginjer Clarke, Joanna Cole, Laura Driscoll, Jennifer Dussling, Jodi Huelin, and Emily Neye

Illustrated by Ron Broda, Pedro Julio Gonzalez, Judith Moffatt, Steven James Petruccio, Cindy Revell, and Mavis Smith

Grosset & Dunlap
New York

Table of Contents

Water

By Emily Neye
Illustrated by Cindy Revell

Water is all around us.

Water can be many things.

Water is rain from the sky.

Water is a puddle
on the ground.

Water is a place to swim.

It is a clear pond.

It is waves in the ocean.

Water is for drinking.

Water is for cooking.

Water is for cleaning.

But that is not all.

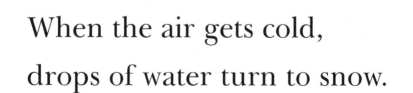

When the air gets cold,

drops of water turn to snow.

When water gets cold,
it gets hard.

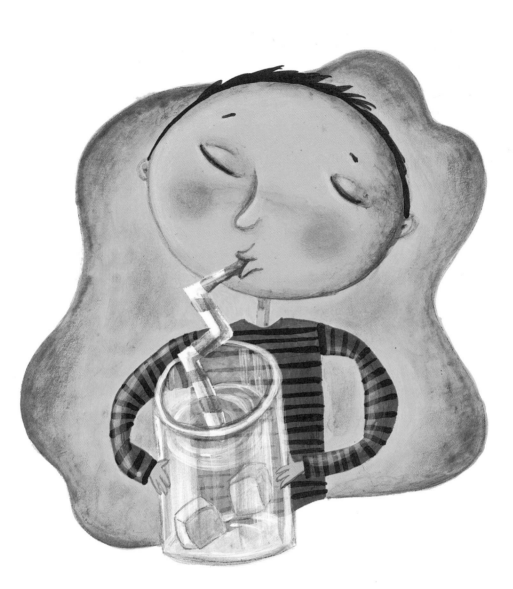

It is ice cubes
in your drink.

It is ice to skate on.

It is icicles to lick.

But water can change.

The sun shines down.
The water turns soft.
It drips and drips.

Now the water is
on the ground.

It is a lake.

It is a stream.

It is water in a well.

But water can change.

When water gets very hot,
it steams and steams.

Now the water is in the air.

30

Steam is tiny drops
of water floating in the air.

A cloud is also tiny drops
of water floating in the air.

But the water does not float
in the air for long.

It gets heavy.

It falls down to the ground.

We call it rain.

Rain or snow,

ice or steam,

it is all water.

Water can be many things.

And water can be fun!

Turtles

By Jodi Huelin
Illustrated by Pedro Julio González

Look over there—
in the water.
Do you see a turtle?

LOGGERHEAD TURTLE

LOGGERHEAD TURTLE

It is a sea turtle.

It has long, strong flippers.

They help the turtle to swim.

Sea turtles are

almost always swimming.

This sea turtle
has come on land.
She is ready to lay her eggs!

LOGGERHEAD TURTLE

She lays her eggs at night.

She lays them in holes.

Then she goes back to the water.

Two months pass.
The eggs hatch one by one.
After three days,
the baby turtles head
for the water.

GREEN TURTLE
HATCHLINGS

Only a few will make it.
Baby turtles are a tasty snack
for birds and animals.

LEATHERBACK
TURTLE

If the baby turtles
reach the water,
they start swimming
right away.

Sea turtles are good swimmers.

Sea turtles are good divers, too.

Some like to dive for jellyfish.

Different sea turtles
eat different things.
Some eat plants.
Like sea grass and seaweed.

GREEN TURTLE

OLIVE RIDLEY

Others eat small creatures.

Like clams and shrimp.

EAST RIVER
COOTER

Turtles need soft food—
they don't have teeth!
They do have <u>very</u> strong jaws.

Turtles also have beaks.
The beaks help them tear food.
Even though turtles
don't have teeth,
they can still bite.

SNAPPING TURTLE

BOX TURTLE

Some turtles live on land.

They are usually called tortoises.

They do not swim.
They only go to water
to drink and take a bath.

You can visit turtles at the zoo.

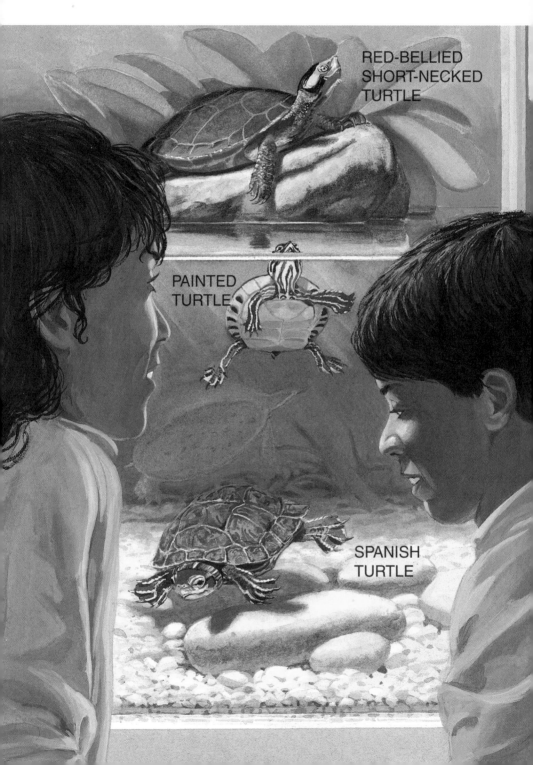

RED-BELLIED
SHORT-NECKED
TURTLE

PAINTED
TURTLE

SPANISH
TURTLE

You can keep some kinds
of turtles as pets.

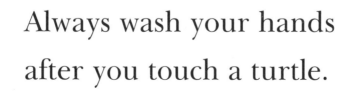

BABY
PAINTED
TURTLE

Always wash your hands
after you touch a turtle.

Sea turtles and land turtles
can live indoors in a fish tank.
Land turtles can also live
outside in a pen.

TORTOIS

You can feed them salad
and flowers and fruits
and vegetables.

Some turtles live
a pretty long time.
Like 30 or 40 years.

PAINTED TURTLE

Other turtles live
a _really_ long time.
Like 70 or 80 years.

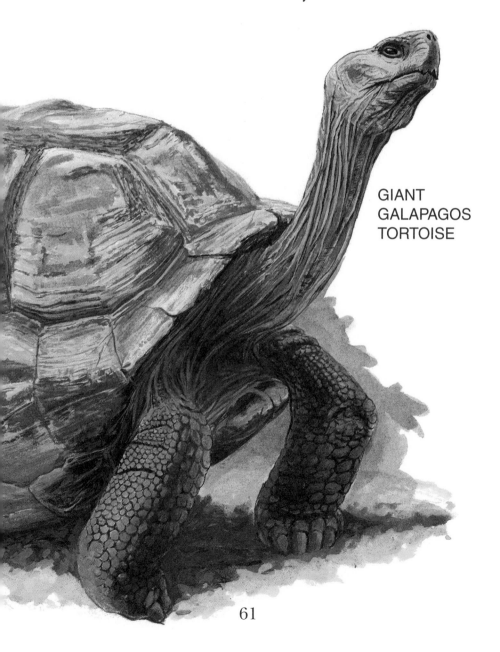

GIANT
GALAPAGOS
TORTOISE

CAR

LEATHERBACK TURTLE

BOG TURTLE

Some turtles are
a few inches long.

LEATHERBACK TURTLE

BOG TURTLE

But some are over six feet long.

That's almost as long as a car!

DESERT TORTOISE

Most turtles have soft bodies
and hard shells.
The shell protects the turtle.
It keeps the turtle's body safe.

Land turtles can tuck
their head and legs
in their shell
if there is danger.
Sea turtles can't do this.

DESERT TORTOISE

GREEN TURTLE

So what do sea turtles do
if there is danger?
They swim away, of course!

STARS

By Jennifer Dussling
Illustrated by Mavis Smith

Look at the night sky.

What do you see?

Lots and lots
of white dots.

Stars!

Long ago
some people said
the sky was like a bowl
turned upside down.
It sat on the tops
of mountains.

The stars were holes—
holes poked in the bowl.

Some people
made up stories
about the stars.

One group of stars
looked like a crown.
People said it was
the crown of a princess.
A god loved the princess.
But then she died.

The god put her crown
in the sky—

so he could see it forever.

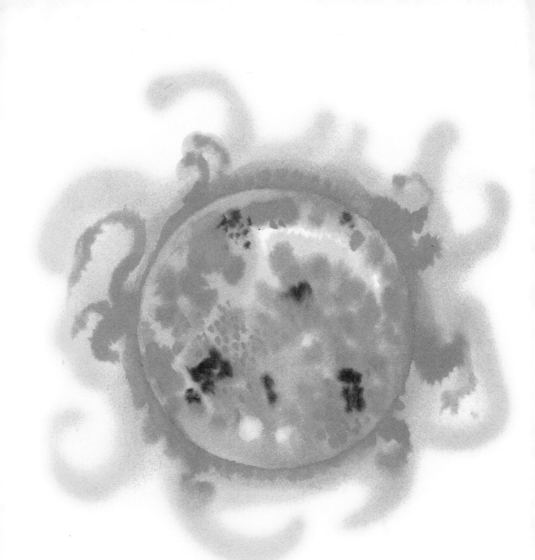

Today we know
what a star really is.
A star is a ball of burning gas.
It is very hot and very bright.

Stars come in different colors.
There are yellow stars
and blue stars.
There are red stars
and orange stars too.

But when you look up
at the sky,
most stars look white.

Star

Earth

Stars are big—
very, very big.
They only look small
because they are
so far away.

Think of the biggest star
and Earth like this.
You have a soccer ball
in one hand.
That is the big star!
You have one little
grain of sand in your
other hand.
That is Earth.

One star is closer
than the rest.
It is not the biggest star.
But it looks big
because it is so near.
We feel its heat.
This star is the sun.

Without the sun,
no plants could grow.
In the day
the sun is so bright
we cannot see other stars.
But they are there
just the same.

Can you ever
see stars in the day?
Yes!

Sometimes the moon
blocks out the light
from the sun.
This is called an <u>eclipse</u>.
(You say it like this: ee-clips.)

There are special ways
to look at an eclipse
without hurting your eyes.

During an eclipse,

the day gets darker and colder.

The stars come out.

And some animals go to sleep.

They think it is night.

But in a few minutes,

the moon moves.

The sun comes back out.

It's day again!

Long ago
sailors used the stars
to help them cross the ocean.

They made
a map of the stars.
It showed them
where they were going.

Stars still help people
find their way.
One group of seven stars
shows which way is north.

These stars look like
different things
to different people.

A bear and three birds.

A hook.

A wagon.

We say it is a big soup spoon.

We call it the Big Dipper.

Look up!

Can you find the Big Dipper?

It's there in the night sky
with all the other millions
and millions of stars.

SPIDER'S LUNCH

ALL ABOUT GARDEN SPIDERS

By Joanna Cole
Illustrated by Ron Broda

It is a hot summer day
in a garden.
Do you see something
in the grass?

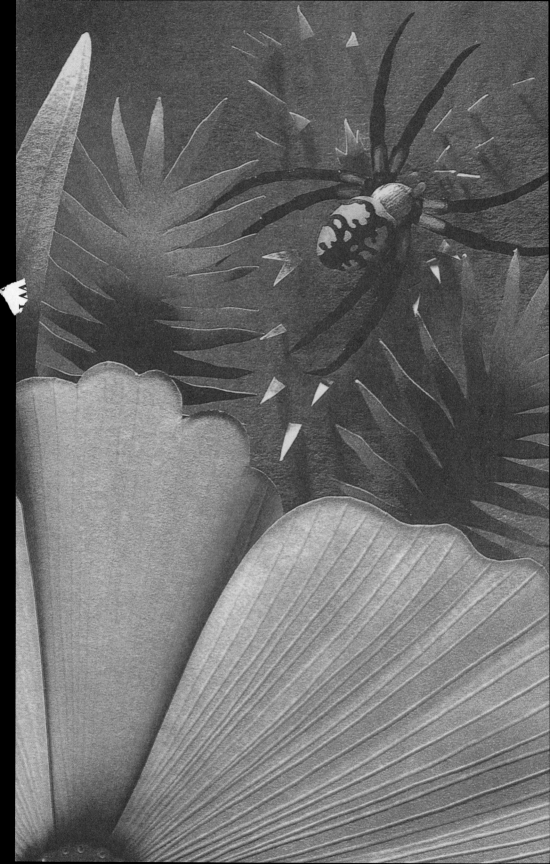

It is a garden spider!
The spider has
lots of legs.
Count them—
one, two, three,
four, five, six,
seven, eight!

From far away

the spider looks small.

But up close

the spider looks big!

The spider has two fangs.

It can bite with them.

The spider has eight eyes.

But it cannot see very well.

eyes

fangs

Now the spider
is ready to eat.
How does she get food?
She catches it in a web!
A long, thin string of silk
comes out of the spider.
The silk is sticky—
like bubble gum.

The spider makes a web—
a sticky web.

Now the web is done.

The spider sits on the web.

She waits for something

to land in it.

Soon a fly flies by.

Zap!
It is stuck—
stuck in the
spider's web!

The fly wiggles.
But it cannot get away.
The spider's web
is too sticky.
The spider cannot
see very well.
But she can feel
the web wiggle.

The spider runs
out on the web.
She bites the fly
with her fangs.

She wraps it up in silk.

Now the fly cannot move.

It is the spider's "lunch"!

The spider eats the fly.

Then she waits.

She waits for something else
to land in her web.

Maybe a little beetle.

Maybe a moth.

Soon a wasp flies by.

Zap!

It is stuck—

stuck in the web!

The wasp makes

the web wiggle—

a lot!

The spider can tell

this is something big!

The spider is not
that hungry now.
She does not want
to eat the wasp.
She walks out
on the web.
She cuts the web
around the wasp.
It flies away.

Tap-tap-tap.
A little male spider comes.
His tapping says
that he is <u>not</u>
something to eat.
The two spiders mate.
Then the male goes away.

Fall comes.
Now the spider is
ready to lay eggs.
She spins more silk.
She is making an egg sac—
a bag to hold her eggs.
The spider's work
is done now.
Soon she will die.

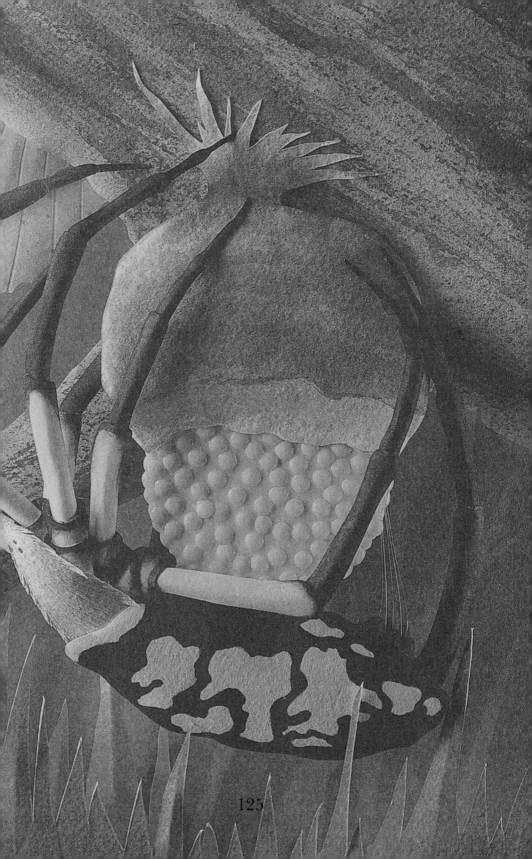

Snow falls.
All winter,
the egg sac waits.

In spring,
baby spiders come out.
Each one climbs up
a blade of grass.
Each one makes
a long silk string.
The wind blows them up.

Each baby spider
finds a new home—
a new place to spin a web.

FROGS

By Laura Driscoll
Illustrated by Judith Moffatt

Ker-plunk!

Something splashes
into the pond.

A frog!

It has strong back legs.

It has webbed feet.

It swims fast.

Frogs feel at home
in the pond.
Why?
Because they begin life
in the water—
as tiny frog eggs.
In the spring,
a mother frog
lays lots of eggs.

The eggs hatch.

Frog babies swim out.

They look like fish.

They swim like fish.

They even breathe
underwater like fish.

But they are not fish.
They are tadpoles.
They will grow up to be frogs.

Soon the tadpoles change.
They get bigger.
They grow little back legs,
then front legs.

And little by little,
their tails shrink
and disappear!

Something also changes
inside them.
Now the baby frogs
can breathe out of the water,
like we do.

The frogs hop onto a log.

They are now land animals.

They still can swim.

But they are not
water animals anymore.

frog

Animals that change this way
are called <u>amphibians</u>.
(You say it like this:
am-FIH-bee-uns.)
Are frogs the only amphibians?

toad

No!

Toads are amphibians, too.

Toads usually have
bumpy skin and shorter legs
than frogs.

There are about 4,000
kinds of frogs.
They live all over the world.
Most frogs are
the size of your hand.

But the biggest frog
is called the Goliath frog,
like the giant.

This picture is about
the same size as the real frog.

Tree frogs are so tiny
they can stand
on your fingertip.
Can you guess
where tree frogs live?
In trees!
Their sticky toes
help them hold on tight!

Sometimes at night
you can hear tree frogs croak.
Lots of frogs croak.
They croak to find mates.

They also croak
to warn other frogs
of danger.
Many animals
like to eat frogs.

But these pretty frogs are safe.
Why doesn't the bird eat them?
Because they have poison
on their skin.

Snakes like to eat frogs.
But this Asian leaf frog is safe.
The snake cannot see it
in the pile of leaves.
The frog stays very still.
Soon the snake goes away.

The barking frog
fools its enemies another way.

It puffs itself up.

Now it looks too big to eat.

But most frogs in danger
do the same thing.
They hop away—fast!

Ker-plunk!

Butterflies

By Emily Neye
Illustrated by Ron Broda

Butterflies live
all over the world.
They are in backyard gardens.

They are in
rainforests far away.

You can find butterflies
on cold mountains...

and in hot deserts.

Butterflies are insects
like flies and ladybugs.
They have six legs,
a body in three parts,
and skin that is hard like a shell.
Like most insects,
butterflies have wings.

There are more than
twenty thousand kinds
of butterflies.
They come in
all different colors.

Butterflies come
in different sizes.
The biggest butterfly has wings
as wide as a robin's wings.

The smallest butterfly
is about the size
of this picture.

But every butterfly
starts out the same way—
as a tiny egg.

This monarch butterfly
(you say it like this: MON-ark)
has just laid
one of her eggs on a leaf.

egg

A few days later,
the egg hatches.
Now it is a tiny caterpillar.

All the caterpillar does is
eat and rest,
eat and rest.
It chews up many leaves.
It grows and grows.

Two weeks go by.
Now the caterpillar
is ready to change.
It finds a safe spot
on a twig or leaf.
It spins a silk pad.
It hangs down from the pad.

It looks as if
the caterpillar is just resting.
But it isn't!
Slowly, it sheds its skin.
Then it forms a hard shell.
Inside the shell,
the caterpillar is changing.

After about a week,
the shell cracks open.
Out comes a pretty
monarch butterfly!

Her wings are wet.
She can't fly yet.
She must let her wings
dry in the sun.

Then the monarch flies
to a bed of flowers.
She is hungry.

Butterflies do not eat leaves
like caterpillars.
They suck sweet juices
from flowers.
Their tongues work like straws.

Some animals like
to eat butterflies.
But these butterflies are safe.
Their wings look like
leaves and bark.
This bird does not see them.
Can you see them?

Are these butterflies?

No. They are moths.

Moths look a lot like butterflies.

But they fly at night.

Butterflies fly in the daytime.

Is this a butterfly?
Yes!
You can tell
because its wings
are closed.

When a moth rests,
its wings stay open.

The summer is ending.
Fall is on the way.

Most butterflies do not
like the cold.
Some sleep all winter.
They find quiet spots,
such as a cave or your attic.

Other butterflies fly south
to warm places.

Monarch butterflies
fly many, many miles.
Clouds of them fill the sky.
In the spring,
they fly back north.
There, they will lay
their eggs.

And soon,
new butterflies will be here.
Maybe some will be
in your backyard!

SHARKS!

By Ginjer Clarke
Illustrated by Steven James Petruccio

Hawaii

It is a hot day.
A surfer waits
for a big wave.

All at once,
something bumps
his board!

Then he sees a fin.

It is a shark!

The surfer swims away.

He is safe.

But he needs

a new board!

Sharks do not bite
people very often.
Surfers look like seals
to hungry sharks.
And sharks love to eat seals.

The most dangerous shark
is the great white shark.

It has a white belly.

It is very big.

Great white sharks eat seals,

fish,

turtles,

penguins,

and even other sharks.

The great white has
many rows of teeth.
Sometimes a tooth breaks.
Then a tooth from behind
takes its place.

Are all sharks dangerous?

No!

The biggest shark
is the whale shark.
It is longer than
a school bus.

The whale shark
eats only tiny fish and shrimp.
It will let a diver
go for a ride on its fins.

basking shark

These sharks
are also very big.

megamouth shark

They do not bite people.
All they eat are
tiny shrimp and animals.

Are all sharks big?

No.

Lots of sharks are small.
This shark is only
as big as a cat.
But it has sharp teeth!

cookie cutter shark

The smallest shark
is about as long as a pencil.
It lives at the bottom
of the sea.
Its eyes glow.
It can see in the dark water!

lantern shark

lemon shark

blue shark

pink goblin shark

There are about
375 kinds of sharks.
They come in many
colors and shapes.

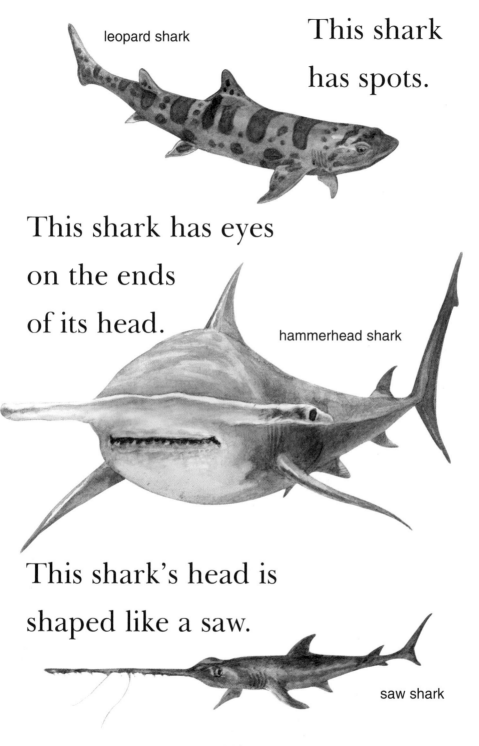

leopard shark

This shark has spots.

This shark has eyes on the ends of its head.

hammerhead shark

This shark's head is shaped like a saw.

saw shark

This shark
is the color of sand.
It is hard to see
on the floor of the sea.
There is fringe
all around its mouth.

wobbegong shark

The fringe looks
like seaweed.
Fish do not see its teeth—
until it is too late!

All sharks are fish.

But they do not have bones.

Their skeleton and jaws
are made of cartilage.
(You say it like
this: car-till-lej.)
Cartilage is strong.
But it bends.
Your ears
and nose
are made
of cartilage.

Like all fish,
sharks have gills.
They breathe water
through their gills.

Like all fish,
some sharks lay eggs.
Shark eggs look
like small purses.
The baby sharks
hatch from the egg cases.

But most sharks
give birth to baby sharks.
Baby sharks are called pups.

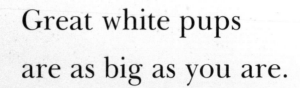

Great white pups
are as big as you are.

The mother shark
does not take care
of the baby sharks.
Right away the pups
start hunting.
They are on their own.

Sharks have been around
for a long, long time.
Before dinosaurs,
there were sharks.

Sharks will be around
for a long time
to come.